The Goodmans Go Camping!

Written by Nancy O'Connor

Illustrated by Lyn Stone

Flying Start
to Literacy®

Contents

Chapter 1
Student of the month   **4**

Chapter 2
Yellowstone, here we come!   **8**

Chapter 3
Setting up camp   **12**

Chapter 4
A smelly nightmare   **20**

A note from the author   **28**

Chapter 1
Student of the month

Cassie Goodman was a good girl. She did her homework on time, was kind and never ran in the halls. Her teacher, Mrs Thompson, had just made her Student of the Month. She couldn't wait to tell her parents!

Cassie's dad, whose name was Ben, often reminded her about how she needed to live up to their family name.

When she showed off her certificate, Dad said, "Wonderful! I know I've told you this before, but when I was a kid, my friends loved to make up jokes about my name."

Cassie sighed. She knew the story by heart. Her dad's friends had often greeted him with a slap on the back, asking, "Hey, have you been good, man?"

"And with a name like "GOODman," Dad said, "it was only natural that I became a police officer. And now, I am the world's best rule follower!"

"Yes, Dad, I know all that, but I can't always be perfect," Cassie said. "Even if Mrs Thompson gave me the award."

She was thinking about the candy bar under her pillow for her bedtime snack and how she'd trampled some flowers along the back fence yesterday when she tried to stop her new puppy, Rowdy, from digging another hole.

"Well, congratulations anyway. We're very proud of you," said Dad.

"In fact," her mum, Laura, chimed in, "we're going on a special holiday when school gets out next week. We're going camping!"

"Yep," said Dad. "We're buying a tent and hitting the road! I was thinking about Yellowstone National Park."

Cassie's eyes sparkled. "In science, we learnt about all the geysers and bubbling mud pots they have there. I'd love to see these things. Can Rowdy come, too?"

"Well, Cassie," Mum said, "I'm sure national parks have rules about pets."

"I promise he'll follow the rules, just like the rest of the Goodmans."

She grinned, then she and Rowdy headed off to bed. She had a new book to read and could almost taste that candy bar!

Chapter 2:

Yellowstone, here we come!

The next night, Mum announced they had reservations at the campground by Yellowstone Lake for the following week.

"Yay!" Cassie shouted. "Yellowstone, here we come!"

"The campground has showers, but our family is only allowed two showers a day. That's one of the rules," said Mum.

"That's easy," Cassie said. "You and Dad can take the showers. Rowdy and I will swim in the lake."

✶ ✶ ✶ ✶ ✶

The drive to Yellowstone took two days, but to Cassie, it seemed like forever. Dad drove exactly the speed limit. Other cars and trucks roared past them on the highway, but he explained that was no reason he should speed.

When they finally pulled up to the entrance to Yellowstone, Cassie saw a park ranger in a guardhouse. The ranger waved and called, "Welcome!"

"Thanks," Dad said. "We have a reservation under the name of Goodman."

The ranger gave Dad directions to the campsite. She handed him a permit for the car's dashboard and an information book.

"Be sure you read this carefully," she said. "Visitors have to follow the rules." She spotted Rowdy in the back behind Cassie.

"Make sure you obey the rules about having dogs in the park, too."

"Ha, ha!" Dad laughed. "We're the best rule followers in the world. They don't call us the GOODmans for nothing!"

Cassie's cheeks grew hot with embarrassment. "Please just give me the book, Dad."

He passed it over the seat. "Look it over while I find our campsite."

Driving through the campground was too interesting for Cassie to read the rule book. She saw caravans and tents, campfires and picnic tables. Some people carried iceboxes and fishing poles down towards the lake.

"Can I read this later?" Cassie asked. "I'm too excited right now."

"Sure," Mum said. "It can wait until after we put up the tent."

Chapter 3
Setting up camp

When Mum and Dad finished putting up the tent, they stowed their sleeping bags and suitcases inside. Mum opened the icebox and got out the lunch.

As everyone ate tuna salad sandwiches, chips and apples, Cassie read the information book aloud. There were a lot of rules:

- No swimming in the hot springs.
- No throwing things into the geysers.
- No imitating elk calls or howling like wolves.
- No hunting or feeding the wildlife.
- Use the toilet facilities, not the bushes.
- Keep all dogs on leashes and pick up after them.

"Some of these rules seem pretty dumb,"
Cassie said. "Who would swim in a hot
spring or howl like a wolf?"

"Some people don't appreciate how special
our national parks are," Mum explained.
"If everyone broke the rules, the parks would
be spoiled."

"Well, I'll read the rest later," Cassie said.
"Can we hike down to the lake now?"
She handed the book to Dad.

On the hike, Cassie spotted a wildflower and reached down to pick it.

"Stop!" Dad said. "There's a rule about that!

He held up the information book and read, "Removing any natural resources such as flowers, seeds, rocks or deer horns is not allowed."

"Not even one little flower?" Cassie asked.

"Yep," said Dad. "Not even one little flower. Remember, we need to be good Goodmans."

Cassie rolled her eyes.

After playing in the lake, fixing dinner and feeding Rowdy, the Goodmans toasted marshmallows over the campfire.

"It's bedtime," Mum said, looking at her watch.

Cassie was so excited about spending her first night in a tent, she wasn't sure she'd be able to fall asleep.

Suddenly, there was a flash of lightning in the distance, followed by a rumble of thunder.

Mum and Dad looked at each other.

"I sure hope that tent is rainproof," Mum said.

As the Goodmans trekked to the bathroom one final time before bed, they heard more thunder. It began to sprinkle. By the time they came out of the building, the raindrops had gotten bigger. Cassie started to laugh.

"This rain may not be a laughing matter, young lady," Mum said.

"It's not the rain, Mum. Look at that!"

She pointed to a sign near the rubbish bins. "DON'T FEED THE SKUNKS," she said. "Who would ever do a thing like that?"

Just then, the sky opened up. Rain poured down.

"Run!" shouted Dad.

By the time they reached their tent, the Goodmans were soaked. They crawled inside, along with their very wet dog, and peeled off their dripping clothes. Everyone put on warm pyjamas.

"Oops! We forgot about the icebox on the table," Mum said. "Ben, you should put that in one of the food storage lockers."

"Laura, I don't want to carry it all the way across the parking lot in the pouring rain. I'll put it in the back of the tent."

Dad hurried out, grabbed the icebox and hauled it inside. Then he took Rowdy's leash and fastened it to one of the tent poles. The dog curled up at the bottom of Cassie's sleeping bag.

As he switched off the torch, Dad said, "Now, let's all try to get a good night's sleep. I hope we stay dry."

Chapter 4

A smelly nightmare

Cassie's eyes popped open. What was scratching on the tent? A bear? A wolf?

Rowdy gave a low, rumbling growl. Cassie lay perfectly still.

"Mum? Dad?" she whispered. Something scurried across her sleeping bag and Cassie gave a loud shriek!

Dad woke up and shouted, "What's wrong?"

The torch's bright beam swung wildly around the tent.

"It's a skunk!" Mum screamed. "Over there!"

Rowdy made a leap for the animal. As the dog lunged, the tent pole he was tied to bent, then snapped. The whole tent came crashing down on the Goodman family, Rowdy AND the skunk.

Cassie was suddenly hit with the worst smell in the world. The frightened skunk had sprayed everything and everybody.

Dad struggled out of his sleeping bag and opened the tent's zippered door. When he did, the skunk scurried past him, out into the early morning light.

Cassie crawled out of the tent, choking from the terrible odour. She thought she might be sick. Mum followed.

"Oh, my word," Mum said, holding her nose. Tears streamed down her cheeks. "What should we do, Ben?"

"Pull Rowdy out, Cassie," Dad said.

"But my eyes are burning. I can't see!"

Dad grabbed Rowdy. "Hurry! Let's get to the bathroom and wash the skunk spray off."

They raced in their pyjamas through the puddles left by the storm. When they reached the open door of the bathroom, Dad stopped short. Cassie bumped right into him.

"What's wrong?" Mum asked.

Dad just pointed. Inside, the skunk huddled under a sink.

"Back out slowly," Dad whispered.

Back at their campsite, Dad got his phone out of his pyjama pants pocket and called the ranger station.

Cassie heard him say, "This is Ben Goodman. I'm sorry to admit I broke a rule."

Then he was quiet, listening to the ranger on the phone.

"Well . . . the one that says not to feed the skunks. We – I mean I – put our icebox in the tent last night. A skunk came in and our dog tried to attack it. The tent collapsed and now we're all covered in skunk spray." He listened again.

"Umm . . . That's a problem. We tried to go wash up, and the skunk is hiding in the bathroom."

Then Dad said, "Okay. We'll see you in a few minutes. Thanks."

When the ranger arrived in her truck, she found the Goodmans in their pyjamas outside their collapsed tent.

"It seems you folks don't know much about camping," she said, shaking her head. "You're lucky it was just a skunk in your tent. A bear would have been much worse."

"We are so sorry," Mum said.

"Well, we caught the little guy and took him out into the woods – where people can't bother him," said the ranger.

She reached into the truck and handed three big cans to Dad. "You go shower now, but first rub this tomato juice all over yourselves. Your dog, too."

"Tomato juice?" Cassie asked.

"Yep," the ranger said, "it won't take all the smell away, but it will help."

"But . . . but . . . aren't we only allowed two showers a day?" Dad asked. "I always – well, usually – follow the rules."

The ranger chuckled. "Well, you can break this rule just one time. After all, most of the time I'm sure you've been GOOD, man."

Cassie groaned, then everyone started to laugh.

A note from the author

Several years ago, in September, a friend and I visited Yellowstone. "Be sure to bring warm clothes," said my friend. "The weather can be very changeable."

I laughed. "That's crazy. Summer is barely over!"

Like the Goodmans, we got a brochure from the ranger at the park entrance. We saw amazing hot springs and geysers. We didn't feed any skunks or howl like wolves. We obeyed all the rules.

That night I told my friend, "Well, we didn't need our warm clothes today after all, did we?"

The next morning, Mother Nature had a surprise for us – 10 centimetres of fresh snow! Sometimes, even she doesn't obey the rules.